HappiMe

Welcome to the first HappiMe book!

HappiMe is a Community Interest Company (CIC) created to help raise self-esteem, self-confidence and happiness levels in children, young people and adults.

HappiMe is a project that we feel very excited and passionate about. If we can help our children understand and gain control of their thinking from a young age, we can save them years of worrying and heartache; resulting in happier, more confident young adults. A child that has the belief that 'I'm not good enough', will more than likely grow into an adult that believes the same. We believe early intervention could very well stop this becoming a self-fulfilling prophecy.

This book is just one of many tools that we have created to help children, young people and adults to stop worrying and be happier.

- The HappiMe App is a brilliant mobile app, which is free for children and young people (small charge for the adult version to keep the kids app free)

- HappiTapping videos are available for free on our YouTube channel. HappiTapping & Finger tapping are simple, yet life changing tools, that children can learn in minutes, to help them handle anxiety and worry.

- HappiMe Mindful and Meditation Bites are designed to help relax and calm children instantly whilst and developing their confidence. Free on YouTube and on the HappiMe App!

We have chosen the font for the text in this book specifically to make it easier for those with dyslexia to read, and have avoided italics for the same reason.

I really hope you and your child enjoy this book and that you use it as a catalyst for lots of future conversations about your "chimps"!

To your happiness,

Jo, Abby and the HappiMe Team xx

HAPPIME

Oscar Meets His Worry Chimp

Meet the HappiMe Characters

Meet the HappiMe Characters

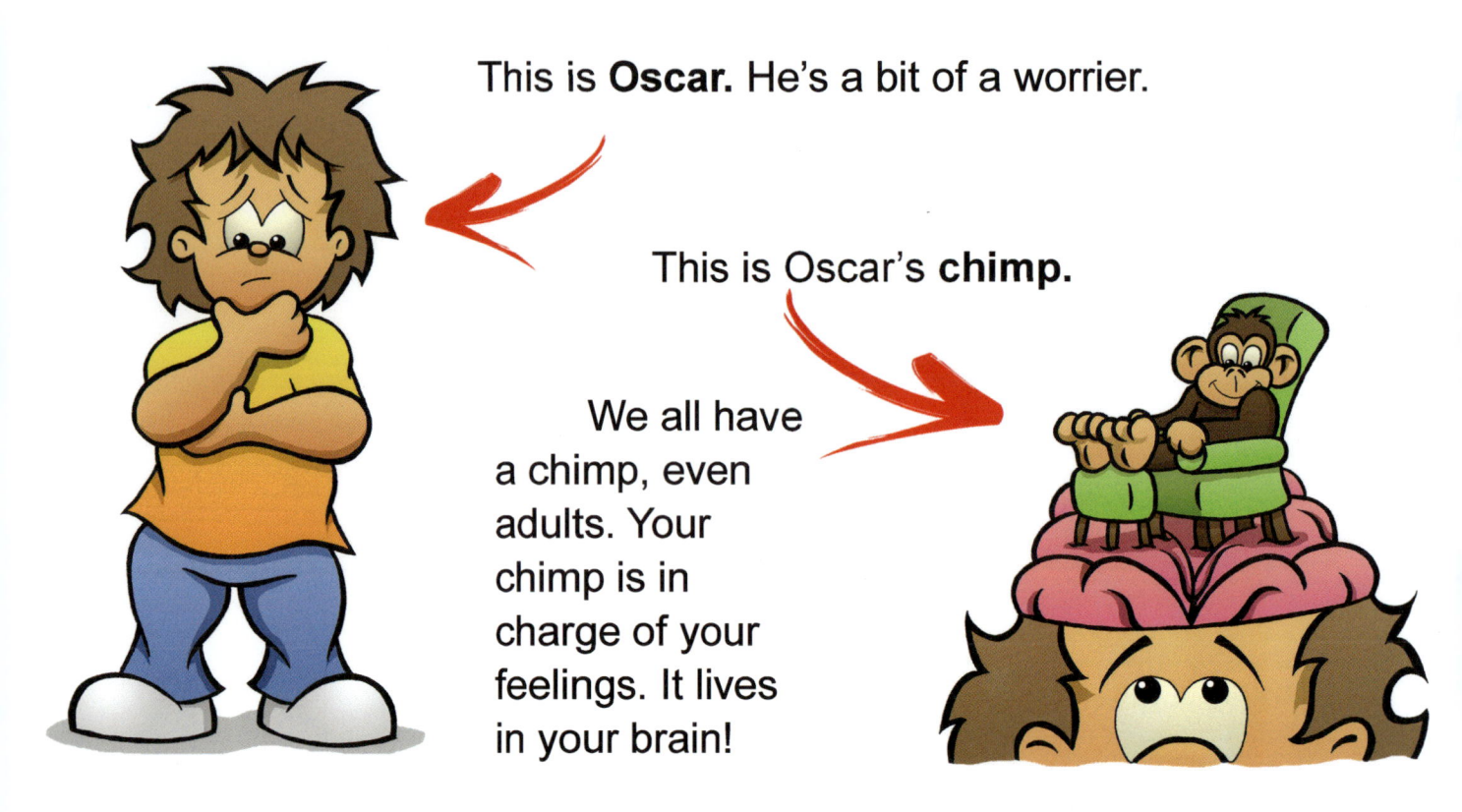

This is **Oscar**. He's a bit of a worrier.

This is Oscar's **chimp**.

We all have a chimp, even adults. Your chimp is in charge of your feelings. It lives in your brain!

Your chimp is often happy, but if it feels scared, it can make you feel worried, sad, upset or angry.

I'm worried about going to school. What if I mess up?

Your chimp means well, but sometimes makes you worry about things you don't need to worry about.

What does your chimp worry about?

And this is Oscar's **HappiTar.** A HappiTar is a Happiness Avatar.

Your HappiTar is the little voice in your head that helps you feel less worried. It makes you feel happier.

It says things like – "you CAN do it" and "there's nothing to worry about".

Your HappiTar is in charge of happiness. It's important to remember that your HappiTar is with you all the time, ready to help you feel better.

What kind of things does your HappiTar say to make you feel better?

There are lots of **HappiTars.** You will meet different ones in other HappiMe books and on the HappiMe App!

Which HappiTar is your favourite?

What does your HappiTar look like?

Lastly, meet your **Computer** Brain.

Your **Computer** stores all your programmes.

When you feel happy, your computer is running the **Happy Programme.**

Some programmes are not as much fun…

What programmes do you think your computer brain could be running in the pictures above?

Now you have met all the characters, let's start reading the book!

Oscar Meets His Worry Chimp.

Oscar was worried. He worried about a lot of things.

He worried that he wouldn't be able to do something new or that he wouldn't be very good at some things.

I can't do it…

What if…?

Oh dear…

New things to do. New things to learn. New places to go. New people to meet. There **always** seemed to be something to worry about!

What kind of things do you worry about?

"**Hello!**" Called a cheerful little voice.

Oscar looked around his room. "**Who said that?**"

"**Oscar, I am over here,**" said the little voice. Oscar looked in surprise at the little HappiTar.

"Who are you?" Asked Oscar. "And... Erm, what are you?"

"I am a HappiTar, your Happiness Avatar. I'm in charge of your happiness!"

"HappiTar?" Thought Oscar, "I didn't even know I had one".

"**Everybody has a HappiTar,**" said the little creature.

"**I heard that your chimp has been giving you a hard time and making you worry about things, so I thought it was about time I introduced myself.**"

A what? What on earth is a HappiTar?

Oscar looked quite confused.

"It's very nice to meet you Oscar," it said.

"To be honest, you are not really supposed to see me," the HappiTar continued.

"I am supposed to be an invisible HappiTar that you can hear and not see, but you seemed so worried about things that I thought I'd better introduce myself!"

"Oh," said Oscar, not knowing what else to say. He was quite sure he wasn't dreaming!

Just then, Oscars chimp appeared.

Hello Oscar!

"HELLO!" called chimp loudly. He bowed slightly. **"Hello Oscar. I am your chimp! I'm in charge of worrying"**

Oscar's chimp started to sing **"There are lots of things to worry about… What if I can't do it? What if I don't like it? What if I'm rubbish at it?"**

There are lots of things to worry about!

What if I can't do it?

"What if I don't like it?"

"What if I'm rubbish at it?"

Oscar was surprised to hear what his chimp was singing, because that was EXACTLY what he was thinking just a few minutes ago.

"Shhh, Chimp!" Said his HappiTar. **"Don't listen to him Oscar."**

Oh dear, what if no one talks to us?

I CAN do this. I'll be fine!

We will be fine. You've worried about parties before and have always had a great time!

PARTY

"There is absolutely no reason why you should be worried. Everyone gets a little nervous when they try something new."

"You don't have to get things right first time. It's OK to make mistakes. Mistakes help us to learn. And everyone makes mistakes sometimes," the HappiTar said. **"As long as we try our best, that's fine!"**

I am always making mistakes!

Me too!

And me!

"So, can you see there is nothing to worry about now?" the HappiTar asked.

Oscar thought for a moment. **"So, it's my chimp who is making me worry? And I can choose not to listen to him and listen to you instead?"** He asked.

"Yes, that's absolutely right!" Said the HappiTar, smiling.

Gertrude?

Bertie?

Frank?

"So Oscar, tell your chimp that everything is OK," said Oscar's HappiTar.

"And now you have met your chimp, you can give him a name. That way you will learn to recognise when your chimp is running the show!"

Oscar thought for a moment. What would he like to call his chimp? He had never named a chimp before!

"Errm… Umm…" he said, thinking hard. **"I know! I am going to call my chimp Charlie. Charlie the Chimp."**

Charlie? I like the name Charlie!

"That's a great name!" Said the HappiTar. **"Now, be firm and tell Charlie the chimp that there's nothing to worry about. He's your chimp so he will only do what you say."**

"OK then," said Oscar.

"Charlie… PLEASE BE QUIET! There is really nothing to worry about!"

Charlie the Chimp stopped what he was doing and looked at Oscar. *"Oh, OK. Don't we need to worry? Phew, that's good!"* He said.

Charlie … PLEASE BE QUIET!

PHEW!

"Well Done!"

"Well done Oscar!" The HappiTar praised with a big smile, **"that was great!"**

"Your cheeky chimp often tells you that things will go wrong. He gets you to worry about things that you shouldn't worry about," it said, smiling at the chimp.

"In fact, he often just makes stuff up for you to worry about!"

My job is to worry!

What would you like to call your chimp?
Your chimp can be a boy chimp or a girl chimp!

BABOO

FLO

MITZY

CHEEKY CHIMP

Oscar was so pleased. Meeting his HappiTar and chimp made lots of sense. He always wondered why he worried so much!

"How do you know Charlie will listen to me next time?" He asked.

"Because each time you tell Charlie the Chimp to be quiet, you are filing it in your computer." The HappiTar replied.

"Your computer lives in your brain, along with Charlie and I," it added.

"My computer?" Oscar was confused again!

"Yes, your computer. Your computer is where your habits are stored." Said the HappiTar.

" Whenever you feel angry, Charlie the chimp will pick the 'Angry Programme' from the computer. If you feel worried, he will pick the 'Worry Programme'. Does that make sense?" it asked.

"I think so," Oscar replied. "And I can train Charlie all by myself?"

"Yes Oscar, that's right," said his HappiTar. **"Each time you tell Charlie to stop worrying, you're training him. When you've done it for a while, he will be trained and the computer will remember to use the new 'I Can Do It Programme'."**

Oscar was amazed. **"It all sounds so easy,"** he thought, **"I am in charge of my thoughts, not Charlie the Chimp".**

He was very glad that he had learned about his chimp, HappiTar and his computer. And what's more, he realised he wasn't worried anymore!

We hope you enjoyed this book!
Find more HappiMe books on Amazon

The HappiMe App is available in the App Store and Play Store. FREE for children and young people.

There is a small charge for the adult version. This will help keep the children's app free forever. HappiMe is a non-profit Community Interest Company (CIC), so any additional profits go towards spreading the HappiMe message.

Adults - please read The Chimp Paradox by Dr Steve Peters. We can't recommend it highly enough!

www.happi-me.org

About Us!

Mother and daughter team, Jo Richings and Abby Pickles, live in South Bristol, UK, where Abby and her brother Sam grew up. They love working together, especially when they get the opportunity to share the stage at talks and workshops. Both are equally passionate about raising self-esteem and empowering others to be the best they can be..

Jo Richings
4 things you might want to know about Jo

1. Jo is fascinated by the way the brain works and has been studying CBT, NLP, Positive Psychology, Neuroplasticity, Meditation, Mindfulness and EFT for over 25 years.
2. She is a Business Coach, Happiness Coach and a Social Entrepreneur who likes to create stuff that makes a difference.
3. Jo is the creator of the HappiMe App, an innovative app aimed and helping children and adults to stop worrying and feel better about themselves
4. Jo has also written a fantastic personal development book called – **"Whoops, there it goes again! How to stay positive when the bottom drops out of your world."**

Abby Pickles
4 things you might want to know about Abby

1. Abby has extensive knowledge in CBT, Psychology, Understanding Learning Difficulties, Understanding Physical and Cognitive Disabilities and working with children in need of special education.
2. She is the lead CYP coach at HappiMe Coaching and offers her unique style of coaching to children and young people who suffer with low self-esteem and confidence issues.
3. Abby works with children and young people both privately and through various schools in Bristol.
4. Abby loves blogging, her rescue dog Bailey and football.

About Us!

Russell Scott
4 things you might want to know about our extremely talented Cartoonist & Illustrator, Russ.

1. Russ is a freelance cartoonist and illustrator based in the UK.
2. He has always been creative and is mainly self-taught. After teaching himself the basics he went on to take evening classes in 3 London colleges where he has learned the finer points of Illustrations and Cartooning.
3. Over the years, Russell has sold his work to the public through craft fairs at London Covent Garden and Greenwich Market. He made the decision to go freelance in 2011 and he has never looked back!
4. You can find him at www.rscottillustrations.com

Printed in Great Britain
by Amazon